THE SAND DUNE TEACHER

by

Clare Chu

For Jerry,
Please enjoy,
With love,
Clare.

9·23·2020.

UnCollected Press

FOR THE FEW

WHO

WALK THE DUNES

WITH ME

These poems are published in the following journals:

Cathexis Northwest Press: "Dreamscape   No. 1" (as "Summer Heat")

Crosswinds Poetry Journal: "The Weightlessness of   Birds"

Rue Scribe: "How To Fry Okra"

The 2River View: "The Raincoat"

The Comstock Review: "The Broom"

The Esthetic Apostle: "The Sand Dune Teacher"

The Raw Art Review: "Denial"

The Raw Art Review: "Nasturtiums"

The Raw Art Review: "Small George"

The Raw Art Review: "Sheep"

The Raw Art Review: "The Lighthouse"

The Raw Art Review: "The Raincoat"

The Esthetic Apostle: "Talisman"

The Perch: "Song of the Trees"

Table Of Contents

I. 1

A LIFETIME, KNEELING...............................1

    SONG OF THE TREES 2

    THE LIGHTHOUSE 3

    THE QUILL...4

    THE RAINCOAT.....................................5

    CURSED 6

    THE DISAPPEARANCE OF BEES.......8

    SMALL GEORGE....................................9

    POSTPARTUM, POSTMORTEM 10

    DREAMSCAPE   No. 1/ No. 2/ No. 3/ (TRIPTYCH) 12

    HOW IT ALWAYS ENDS   (TANKA) 14

    SHOUTING DOWN THE VEIL 15

    HAIKU 16

    HOW TO FRY OKRA 17

    DREAMSCAPE   No. 4 18

    THE SHELL OF A WALNUT LOOKS LIKE A BRAIN 19

    FIRST LINES..20

    HOME...21

    BE WATER 22

    THIS MORTAL COIL............................24

    DENIAL 26

    INSTRUCTIONS FOR MY DEATH.......28

II. 31

THE END OF THE ROAD, SO FAR AHEAD...........31

   THE SAND DUNE TEACHER 32

   THE CLOUDS SEND DOWN RAIN 34

   THE FALCON MUMMY......................................36

   NASTURTIUMS..38

   DAMAGED GOODS...39

   MISSING SAN MIGUEL 40

   HERE SHE REMAINS WHERE IT MATTERS
   LEAST...41

   DREAMSCAPE   No. 5 46

   ANOTHER SHADE OF GREEN..........................47

   SHEEP 48

   JUNE MORNING   (TANKA).............................49

   THE WEIGHTLESSNESS OF BIRDS 50

   THE BIRTHDAY PARTY, 1944 52

   SNOWBOUND IN JERUSALEM.........................54

   TALISMAN 55

   TEXTING 56

   COLD SNAP 57

   YOU ARE NOTHING..58

   THE BROOM..60

   SOMEDAY I'LL LOVE CLARE CHU 62

THE SAND DUNE TEACHER

I.

A LIFETIME, KNEELING

SONG OF THE TREES

This morning I put
a bag of pistachios in the oven,
misplaced my wedding ring,
but no matter.

In my garden,
a scarlet butterfly lies
comatose on the grass
under silver trees —

the trees, I think they sing to me —

their sunlit leaves tumbling into
my dragged-through-the-hedge-backwards hair,
as I deadhead the roses.

This afternoon
listening to Ella,
I will bake peach cobbler,
let it cool by a glass of ruby wine.

And when the song of the trees
is surrendered to the rising moon,
and when stars fall into
my outstretched hand,

then I will remember you.

THE LIGHTHOUSE

*The Guyanese coast is dotted with islets, on one of which stands
a lighthouse named Enfant Perdu, the Lost Child of the Guyana Penal
Colony. It is not the only French lighthouse thus named, but it is the
most solitary.*

I am the keeper of your light —
tu es mon enfant perdu.

I tend to you with hands
that burn the wick, palms

scorched with oil, hands
that polish the once-blind lens.

I measure the savage wind
that surrounds you,

I strive under every moon
that severs your infinite beam.

I tend to you always —
you, who devours me.

You, my servant,
yet I kneel before you.

Your pulse comes
and goes.

You, stalwart, of safe harbor,
you, keeper of vast waves.

Have mercy.

THE QUILL

We tie squares of burlap over our shoes. No one can hear us as we creep across the cobbled yard, climb over the gate and into the field. It is not our land.

Hidden in shadows, the evening is still. I unwrap the burlap, remove your shoes to warm your feet and whisper, *I want you to bend me like the wind against the grass. Take me and change my shape. Cradle me as you unfold me. Kiss me as though it's a punishable act. Let your tongue wet the lids of my eyes. Press stars into my palms until you see blood. When you moan, let me hear the lowing of cattle.*

You take off my clothes. We lie down on the ground. Through stands of birches, the waxing moon shines silver on a feather in the dirt. You whisper to me in one ear, *Turn over. I want to write.*

The salt of your tears stings as the quill cuts into my shoulder blade. Your every sigh cuts me open. You whisper to me in my other ear, *Turn over,* then use the feather to brush dry earth from my parched lips.

Together we watch my blood dry on the tip of the quill.

THE RAINCOAT

Once I could dance on a blade of grass,
my feet could melt stone —

now I am pinned down by earthbound clouds.
I thought I had eternity all buttoned up,

then you borrowed my raincoat, wore it daily,
left it billowing in the wind.

In its pockets I hid the bullets I took for you,
tendrils of time I lost, knowledge shucked along the way.

The shelter of my freedom.
Before the rain came, I tried to call out,

but my throat was stuffed with ash,
in that moment I knew —

dying of fright is an actual thing.

CURSED

This is the first time I leave my body:

I look down at the child, sapling slender,
her big brother running away with the wind
as arms flapping, an old man flies

across the field, grabs the child,
snatches her shoe, tears it from her foot,
five pink toes stand in spiked grass.

In her hands, crushed in fear,
wild white lilies
shot through with purple veins.

The man looms over her, his onion breath
streams into her wide, shocked mouth.
She clamps it shut, swallows in one crucifying gulp

a lifetime of another's crackling pain.
The air stops, the birds are silent,
heads bow in prayer or shame or horror.

We watch, the child and I —

he fills her shoe with dark earth,
one wet worm caught in the pile,
then stoops over her, drops the shoe,

hisses:
Get out, this is my field, my grass, my flowers, my sun.

This is the first time I leave my body,
O but not the last —
I return to save myself.

THE DISAPPEARANCE OF BEES

We tumbled hand-in-hand
through poppy fields through
clover and sweet-pea meadows

drowsy bees flirting above us
you tracing a golden path

of fallen pollen from
my throat to my heart

this is how flowers have sex
your words slow

dripping honey
into the comb
enfolded in wet grass.

*

Quietly without notice
the bees have disappeared
their colonies collapsed

loyal queens long gone
days once melting with love
now tick tick tick — over.

*

SMALL GEORGE

My mother said not to play near the old well, but she didn't say a thing about playing in it. We were all there, even Big George, on the blistering summer day that Small George fell into the well, never to be seen again, like Alice-down-the-rabbit-hole, minus enchantment. In the heat of the moment, we made a blood-brother pact to deny our part in his death, and to this day our parents believe that Small George wandered off from the group and, unobserved, fell headlong into the deep well. The magnolia trees were in full bloom that day; their heady fragrance made us delirious, we decided to see how far we could put our heads down the well without lifting our feet off the ground. Small George was the shortest, so we turned a blind eye to his dangling feet, as long as his head went down there. He was crying that day, we made him fill his mouth with pebbles and drop them into the well one by one, while we listened long and hard to them plopping into the water. It was an initiation ritual, we had all done it at one time or another. Immediately we knew he hadn't survived his fall. In subsequent years when magnolia blossoms gave off the first scent of summer, I would walk to the well. One-year Big George was ahead of me, standing there alone. I stood next to him. *What are you doing here,* I asked? *I don't know*, he shrugged, *it seems like the most peaceful place to be.*

POSTPARTUM, POSTMORTEM

I told them
the phone rang,
loud, unexpected —
demanded my attention.

I left you splashing in the bath
to answer the call.

I told them it was an accident,
not sure how it happened.

Grave-silent,
the phone did not ring,
did not beckon
that evening.

*

I watched you play,
sang a lullaby,
smiled at you and to myself.
Then pulled you under,
held you down.

Your hands reached out,
I cupped your head,
washed your curls,
closed your eyes,
unfolded your fingers.
We lay together —
limp and cold,
waiting to be found,
your body swaddled,
my heart cocooned.

*

DREAMSCAPE   No. 1/ No. 2/ No. 3/   (TRIPTYCH)

Amber shadows stretch over a malachite pond.
I have no friends left under the wilted lotus.

The price of staying is much too high.
A breeze that beckoned me is long gone.

If I went into the hills I could enjoy seclusion —

but for now, I can only guess
where the ducks hide their dreams.

*

In the desert there is nowhere to hide my dreams,
only the ready spines of cacti on which to hang them.

My dreams are the whiff of fires blazing in the hills,
my dreams are flowers that bloom but once under night's cover.

*

Come nighttime I tuck my dreams
under lavender pillows I chose
against your steel-gray walls.

Husband,
if you'd wanted me to dream of you,
you'd have painted our room
a more delicate shade
than your gunmetal-gray.

*

HOW IT ALWAYS ENDS   (TANKA)

It was the last time
Your hands on my throat choked me
Words stayed inside me
Your kiss made me gasp for air
This is how it always ends

I woke in the night
Hail bounced off the tiled roof
Leaving our cold bed
I threw open the window
Wanting to breathe in the storm

All of a sudden
A two-hundred-year comet
Streaking through the stars

I almost woke you to watch
Your death mask roaring by me

SHOUTING DOWN THE VEIL

After Forugh Farrokhzad, Wind-Up Doll

Do not dive inside my heart.

I was young once.
I was your lover.
I laugh at the absurdity.

My mind chose sex one day.
My body became sex one night.

My life is an open window.
You stand outside.
You were a god.

You are a boy.
You love — like a boy.

I forgive you.
I forgive anger.
I forgive sex.

My tears are invisible.
My shame is splendid.

My eyes meet yours.
I reach into your mouth.
Silence your voice.

I am shouting now.

HAIKU

Pull to open it
Fire Gloves Fire Extinguisher
No smoke without fire

HOW TO FRY OKRA

Last weekend, Sabiqah couldn't gather her words,
reluctant to admit that she was homeless again,
that their 'Welcome' mat was covered by a blanket of ash,

that her husband Frank came home
from the hospital after his third stroke
with a hankering for fried okra,
just like his MeeMaw made,

and that she refused him,
because she was angry he'd been back to hospital,
because in Bangladesh she'd always made Dharosh Bhaji,
because this was the South — his home,

that Frank was petulant with her,
went downstairs to the empty apartment
where her mother, lately converted, newly passed,
had lain for a week in the scorching heat,

that he fried a skillet of okra,
dipped in buttermilk, dredged in cornmeal,
managed to set the pan alight,
poured water on flaming peanut oil,

and with enthusiasm — or so it seemed to Sabiqah —
burnt their house down in its entirety.

DREAMSCAPE   No. 4

I stood
at the lake
dreaming
chilled by
the mist
watching it
catch and
drift away

I should
have stayed

I would
have been
myself
not
the wound
forever
unbound

THE SHELL OF A WALNUT LOOKS LIKE A BRAIN

It's not a punishment, Father says, as we pull up to Grandma's house. He stares ahead, hands on the wheel, idling in the drive. I see Grandma standing out front. The door has been painted dark-green since my last visit, it makes the leaves on her skirt disappear.

She is waiting for me, hands folded as if in prayer. She must have missed church this morning. Grandma doesn't smile ever. Her eyes look beyond the car at the walnut tree. Last month she promised we will pickle walnuts together.

When they ripen.
If I've been good.

Go on then, Father says, *trot along, I'll see you next Sunday*, he touches my shoulder, coughs. As I climb from the car Grandma turns, goes into the house. I walk to the dark-green door, fix my smile to my face. Before I follow her in, before I turn and wave,

Father drives away.

FIRST LINES

Me, in your kitchen, leaning against the marble counter, tracing
never-ending veins on its surface with my thumb.

You, flipping poems on the griddle, lost in time, staring out over
the stucco wall, absently humming a song I know, so full of soul
— it makes me want to sing with you.

What will it be, you ask softly, *you want your poem over easy or
sunny-side up?*
But neither would suit me this morning —

for I want a poem of first lines
                       Last night I dreamt I went to Manderley again

a six-minute poem
                     I shut my eyes and all the world drops dead

a cascade of words
               Death is a Dialogue between the Spirit and the Dust

carefully selected
                               I can not walk

as only you know how
                   Give me back my broken night

I lift my thumb from the smooth stone. You smile and say,
Maybe I'll poach a pantoum for you today.

HOME

Walk with me through the ochre wood
to the foothills, to our old place,
its crumbling bricks riven
by lichen, by morning glory.

Come with me over the stone wall,
where once-tame lavender
and thyme have laid waste
to the relic of our home.

All that's left — a threadbare carpet
held down by the night's first stars,
chipped cups to catch rainwater
for the birds,

fistfuls of dust that sift and curl
like smoke
through our pallid hands.

BE WATER

My mother always said, *I will die by water.*
Did she mean 'beside' or 'in', as in 'under'?

It was cancer of the brain that took her
in the early hours after the hospice-nurse
informed me she was hanging on
by a single thread just to stay with me.

I take her hand as she dies —
through the window I watch snow fall
sideways, not sticking, turning to slush.

A week later, unknowing, my teacher says,
There are swimmers and sinkers in this world
and you, Clare, are a sinker.

After how many times sinking
do you hold yourself down?

Outside my classroom the snow still falls.
I open a textbook and write below the title:

'I will be buried in a cemetery under the snow'

My mother's gift to me.

THIS MORTAL COIL

Muriel is on her deathbed.

Her hand rests in mine,
transparent, light as paper.
        Darling girl, don't leave me, she rasps,
her voice speckled
like dusty parchment.

Muriel dreams of birthday wishes from the Queen.
My aunt was born during the Great War, 1917,
the year the Palace dispatched its first centenarian telegram.

In World War II, she drove an ambulance
brimful of downed pilots,
        in pieces, faces burnt,
            irretrievably scarred.
She doesn't remember,
or has chosen to forget.

Her brother, a bomber pilot, long since gone,
went to war one person — overwhelmed by death
he returned as another.
With thanks, the Queen knighted him
for his service to the Potato Marketing Board.

Talk to me, Muriel pleads from her bed.
Outside the window, a host of swallows
is heaven-bound on spiraling air.
> *I want to hear your beautiful voice,* she says
> *before I shuffle off this mortal coil.*

The nurses leave the windows cracked
> to encourage in any passing angel,
> to release the odor of death.
Yet they keep my aunt alive
day after bloody day.

Before teatime she drifts into sleep,
I feel her hand tremble in mine as she dreams.
She is carefully changing gear,
not wanting to distress
the shell-shocked pilot lying behind her.

She doesn't recognize her brother,
>   or refuses to see
instead, she murmurs faintly to me,

> *Darling girl, I have to go now.*

DENIAL

I am not your killer.

I did not wait for you under the steel-gray moon in the park as you cut through the avenue of cypress trees that Thursday after choir practice at St. Mark's. I never heard you nervously humming Verdi's Requiem in time to your heart's cleaving beat, your performance only days away.

I didn't see your weary face, midnight eyes cast down, hands thrust deep in your pockets, blond hair straying from a silken scarf worn like a death wish around your throat.

*

I read that you were found in underwear and gloves, velvet limbs bound with black rope, facing a tree, wrists tied as though in prayer, your knees jammed into its spreading roots, its branches lifting to heaven.

I could only imagine you begging for mercy as the world dissolved around you, as your tears soaked the leaves beneath you — that you were not found wanting as you fell into the darkness.

*

As silence spread like ash on a dying fire, I prayed for you to intercede for me, that what was hidden be revealed, that no sin remains unavenged. I asked for absolution, though the righteous are unsafe, though the faithful endure the pains of hell.

Lamb of God, who takes away the sins of the world, deliver me from the deep pit.

Lamb of God, who takes away the sins of the world.

Lamb of God.

Lamb.

INSTRUCTIONS FOR MY DEATH

Open the shades.
I want to see the heavens
          gaping through
a sky of whitecap clouds.

Open the windows,
look for a croft of swallows
          sweeping over
silver-blue waves.

Let me hear Elgar's cello concerto —
the 1965 Jacqueline du Pré version.
I love the dread in it,
you love the passion —
          my elegy.

You can dispatch me during the first movement
before the bassoons kick in.

I know what you think,
I've always known what you think.
          I can't do this. I can't be the one.
          I've seen too much in my life for this.

You are the only one who can.

We were both of sound mind when we agreed.
Choose the pillow carefully, I'm allergic to down
          — but you know that.
Not the one on the piano stool —
          too compact,
I don't want to go out with a black eye.

Ignore my fingers
        plucking at the brittle sheets.
Ignore your thoughts
        of bad karma.
You always were a slipshod Buddhist.

        Don't hesitate —
you've never been one to hold back.
        Kiss my forehead —
let your lips linger for a moment.
        Don't choke —
my dear, don't cry.

Keep your eyes on the swallows,
on the morning moon.

I will be waiting,
and you are not long coming.

II.
THE END OF THE ROAD,
SO FAR AHEAD

THE SAND DUNE TEACHER

I watch my teacher
ahead of me —
he walks
      up and
      down
the lambent dunes.

Sand trails from
the hourglass of his hand.
We've walked
      so far
      I can't
recall his face.

Weariness sits,
      a shroud
on his shoulders.

Even so,
I don't expect him
      to pause
      mid-dune —
he never pauses
      mid-dune —
and half-turn
toward me.

Sand whips my cheek.
His few words
           suffocate
the arid air.
He is leaving.

He can no longer
walk the dunes
           with me,
           with anyone,
let alone by himself.

He sinks
into the quicksand
of the coming dusk.

There is a raw moment,
           a fissure,
before   I start
to walk
           up
           and down
the flickering dunes,
chasing the fireflies
ahead of me.

THE CLOUDS SEND DOWN RAIN

on the studio
where
     running
         water
is used as a
     pillow
it should be easy to dream
of nothing

but I am twisted up
restless in my retreat
turned
     inside
       out
as I lay my head down
thoughts
tumble like water
       over
         stones

and I wonder what
the Master
      in the Garden
            at the Edge
                 of the Universe

thinks
as he sits under a tall pine tree
watching
      the rain
          fall

THE FALCON MUMMY

after Pablo Neruda, One Hundred Love Sonnets: XVII

There are days when a look from you sears me,
days when my questioning glance fans the flames,
days when I yearn to climb outside the tinderbox.

To quell the risk of being consumed by you,
I keep the body broken,
                              the heart embalmed.

                    *

My cat left headless birds, half-dead field mice,
the occasional lizard on my bed. She taught me
to hunt. Prey-driven, she took my tongue,
                              stole my night vision.

When she was killed, hit by a car —
I wrapped her in white cotton,
laid her down beside me.

                    *

For you, I save blue chamomile blossoms, rutile crystals,
                Da Hong Pao tea, champaca oil.

My words — your words.   Parceled in Yuzen paper.

On days when I am muted, even Neruda — with his arrow
of carnations, topaz, rose of salt — provides no salve.

                    *

'To flee' can be twinned with 'fleeting'.
Old English:
flee — fleon: *"to take flight, fly from, avoid, escape,*
...drive away, banish".
fleeting — fleotende: *"floating, flying, moving swiftly,*
...existing only briefly".

*

You are never so close that your hand, never so close
that your eyes. In this form in which I am not,
bind me with Egyptian linen so I can be

Falcon.

*

NASTURTIUMS

You can plant, grow and care for nasturtiums in the meanest soil, they're not choosy. Although that doesn't matter one iota if you are a three-star *Michelin* chef that has his petals delivered daily, fresh, and on ice. It doesn't matter that it is the easiest flower to grow from seed, nor that the seeds are large and can be held by not-so-nimble fingers. This makes them a fitting first plant for children who will revel in their saffron, rose and crimson colors, who will, with urgency, pull their mothers down to the soil to smell a single flower.

That has grown up almost overnight, and holds a subtle fragrance which will never clash with chilled pineapple parfait drizzled with warm mango coulis. And the worldly *bon vivants* who love to eat in the 'Top 100 Restaurants In The World' will hardly notice that the petals on their forks will melt in their mouths with a sweetness and a spicy radish-like after-kick. Because unlike the child who listened to her flower growing, they did not heed their deadpan waiter serving dessert. They did not hear the small whispers of their hearts. And the child's mother, who thankfully saw sense in a Seventies world, called her Rose after another sweet, edible flower (noting that it had thorns for protection).

Rather than Nasturtium — because who could ever spell it correctly or wants to be saddled with the nickname Nasty? She crouches down with her only child and says, *try it, you can eat it*, not understanding Rose at all when she whispers,

Mother, I can't eat this flower that I have grown myself.

DAMAGED GOODS

"Shame is the lie someone told you about yourself." — Anais Nin (attributed)

At seven years old
my freedom tossed aside
by your presumption
that I shouldn't mind it.

By your assumption
that gold-wrapped chocolates
in a box tied with a bow
would appease me.

By your arrogance
that I wouldn't tell —
because how could I
know the words to use?

You can rest assured
that I put on a show,
wishing help was on the horizon,
while praying it wouldn't come —

the secrets I've kept are shards of ice
scattered through my blood,
they drop into their chambers —
the interminable spin never spent.

MISSING SAN MIGUEL

And the weft of the melting
and the weave of my heart-break

are not at all like our mornings
with their swift scent of lavender
                    and darkly brewed coffee.

HERE SHE REMAINS WHERE IT MATTERS LEAST

1.

She tries to remember
a white picket fence
roses climbing over it

The fence is living
grown taller each year
now dressed with mildew
embedded with nails
to keep the roses   standing

She can see but only just
slivers of
                        sky-blue sky
poking through
ever-narrowing slats

                fence
        the   will
  Soon   grow
     a roof of thorns and tight buds
            she will be in a
            /house-cage-house/
                of her own
                home-making

She has let this happen

2.

In late summer   she dreams
the wind takes charge
blows   it   all   away
into the open fields —
her /house-cage-house/

She won't rush to stop it

3.

In late summer she has
nowhere to be
she is at the water's edge
on the border
of wet sand – dry sand

The tide has gone out   left behind
blind albino crabs tangled
in strands of seaweed

She unravels the seaweed   watches the crabs   run

Seaweed grows in the warmth of the sun

She sorts her seaweed
into long strips
it glistens on the sand
She weighs it down
at one end with
                    a stone
begins to braid it

long luminous ropes
slip with ease through her hands
she is untethered

Her hair thinned with the years
she loops the seaweed around her neck
hooks onto her ears   over her head

makes hair

Walks back to her /house-cage-house/
(that is not there)
in her pockets she carries sea glass
duller with each   step away
from the ocean.

Her seaweed braids are tie-bobbed in her hair
She dreams   she brushes —
strokes   it   into   long   strips

She is windblown
back to wet sand – dry sand
pushed into the ocean

She finds round pebbles to put
with the sea glass in her pockets
to weigh her down   turn back the tide

to no avail

//She should have built a seawall to protect herself//

4.

She dreams   her lungs crave air
she is twisted Juniper driftwood

She sleeps on heaving seas
splintered   blind-sided
by the moon
she cannot change course

No longer buoyant wood
she is sea-foam lilting
further   and   further   away

5.

Without arms how does she propel herself
through water?

6.

Come morning she is thrown
onto wet sand – dry sand
she dreams   she can breathe again
in and out   in and out

She wakes late in the day
she stands motionless

7.

The thorns are thick
The buds are closed

DREAMSCAPE   No. 5

The past is a dream
from which we awaken
each morning.

The space between us
is both infinite and finite.

With a brush of my hand
I open you.

With a brush of your hand
you close me.

ANOTHER SHADE OF GREEN

My wounds were already deep when in my troubled sleep you came at me armed with a mace and staff. Then in the morning half-light I woke with the sun and watched it trip and fall through the open window into our room, where the air never moves.

I have a fear of twisted shapes that shift in the dead of night when I feel helpless and blind.

Daylight was safe until now, but with the sun cut into sharp pieces it was time to leave. I gathered it up, cradled by my body and escaped out of the window into the olive tree you planted too close to the house.

I know this tree, the snap and crackle of each leaf, every strong upward branch. Last summer you forced me to forage there, to harvest ripe olives for you, to shake them into your bitter arms. I climb as far as I can to the upper boughs where a few olives remain.

In this lofty place, I miss you. I remember us as better. Yet our love was always more monstrous than ideal. When we met, your eyes were the color of an owl's wing, now they are a land of flat shadows.

I carry the sun warm and heavy in my arms. In some cultures, blue is just another shade of green, and here tree and sky merge. Too much happened to us down there. I feel the pulling clack of leaves, take one long breath and leap into another shade of green.

Only then I look back at what I've left behind, the common decay of everyday life. You.

SHEEP

Finally, I made a decision to leave my job in the billing department to become a shepherd. Not that there was much call for shepherds, but someone had to be accountable for the sheep that were suddenly present on the freeway overpass. Each morning as I drove to work, I would see one more sheep looking over the barrier, wondering where the cars were going. Sometimes at night, I lay awake counting sheep. My mother taught me to do that when I couldn't sleep. It didn't help. There seemed to be more sheep than numbers when I was a child. Far better to gaze through the skylight at stars, until my eyes closed. I always thought that was why I became an accountant, because I felt satisfied balancing numbers instead of counting sheep. Later in life, I am drawn to be with sheep more and more. Once they started appearing, I felt called to care for them, to tend to my growing flock.

JUNE MORNING   (TANKA)

stop — listen
to the hummingbird
beating wings
hiding in bamboo
show yourself to us

in pale dawn
fallen by your side
I am you
laughing drinking tea
sunlight in our hair

dreaming hearts
unlikely soul mates
mourning time
we leave together
cold tea in the pot

THE WEIGHTLESSNESS OF BIRDS

I'll be talking with you,
my rare and sacred friend,

when I draw my final breath,
no different from the one before —

at first, you may not notice
the thinning veil of my life,

but I trust you'll check
the pause in our conversation

about the weightlessness of birds

and shoot me your
hang on a moment look,

one eyebrow raised —
I haven't finished yet.

Because, as I'm leaving, you
will need to instill in me

the gravitas of how birds circle
on rising columns of thermal air,

how I soon will soar even higher
than the frozen lark we found by the lake,

where long-gone souls still themselves
in the slant of frosted moon-shadow.

Now we sit in our slumbering house
where soon enough we'll rest together,

and let the rough edge of salt
burn around our eyes.

THE BIRTHDAY PARTY, 1944

I didn't want to go to the party. I didn't know the birthday girl. It was across the river. Janos, my brother came. Jani, my escort — dashing and wild. With panache, he played the piano for the birthday girl. She looked down. I examined a newly-minted stain on her blush-white frock. The notes faded. I felt the rumble of faraway planes. The fluttering wings of moths, so easily crushed or burned. We held our breath, then blew out ten candles on her cake. German soldiers blew up our bridges. Balls of fire sizzled in the water. Insistent, loud, furious. Dividing Budapest into Buda and Pest. No-one went home until the river froze. Until we could walk on the ice.

Germans within, Soviets without. The noose ever tightening. The servants gone. Mamma couldn't pay them, couldn't feed them. Only Marta stayed. Her whiskers tickling my neck, she kissed me each night. She had forgotten where she came from. She had no place to go. My parents' precious horse, Nimrod, was put out to pasture. No racing, no flying past cheering crowds. No thrills for them in the winner's enclosure. Eaten later by a Soviet general loath to dine on his own horse. Mamma was in denial. The Red Army overran the city. Marta hid Janos and me in the cellar. Fists in our mouths. Dismal, dark, but safe she thought.

Stomping in the house. Shouts on the stairs. The smell of war. Fat, bald. *What have we here?* Hands grabbing. *Look at you.* Fear. *Yuri, leave her, too young — no breasts.* Jani cries, *I'll give you my watch, Patek Philippe, my father's.* Defender of mankind. *We'll take them both.* Hands on me. Grimy fingernails. Voracious fingers inside me.

I look out through the broken window. On the ledge, a fly is trapped in the dust, one leg shaking. Nearby, mothers scream from the shell-shocked tombs. Over the bloated cemetery, the sinking fog is blind.

SNOWBOUND IN JERUSALEM

In Tel Aviv, looking out
towards the beach, watching
empty waves
like the Banzai Pipeline
crashing on the shore.
Yesterday,
in the early afternoon I came
from Jerusalem
where snow was due to fall.
The sky was packed full, though
you can never rely on that.
Flying home
Tel Aviv to Oahu,
I could have been
snowbound in Jerusalem.

TALISMAN

When I started to choke on the plastic baby Jesus in the fruit cake
(who was lost by now to those with no faith and even less luck), a
nearby friend thumped me soundly between my shoulder blades,

forcing me to vomit Jesus into my glass of Chateau-Neuf-Du-
Pape, where he floated languorously on his back until I retrieved
him, licked his little naked white body clean as a whistle,

remembered the restaurant was a convent back in the day, and
with a smidgeon of guilt shoved him into my jacket pocket, where
he languished forgotten, until one winter morning

when I felt my own body melting into the thin ground like Main
Street in some suburban town the morning after a squall when the
plough trundles through, parting the drifting snow.

Baby Jesus was given a chance at redemption, and I, ever
optimistic for my own, transferred him from pocket to handbag
where he now communes with a miniature jade pig and a glass
vial of glitter stars.

.

TEXTING

Without fail,
when I return to you
I erase your words.

My finger hesitates over 'delete'
as if I'm removing
a part of you.

I hope
you have kept
all of my texts.

COLD SNAP

I am not one of your broken birds to be rescued,
carried inside laid out on linen in a worn-out box,

tended to daily until you deem I can fly once more.
I would rather fend for myself dragging a wing

canted   at   an   awkward   angle,   my   body   slant,
graying   against   the   slow - to - startle   winter   snow.

I hear all you well-meaning souls you mutter
to yourself and to the few you hope will listen

poor things I should snap *your* necks cleanly,
end *your* misery quickly bury *you* under the ice.

YOU ARE NOTHING

I am naked
I sink to the floor
Water pools on the tile
The shower is running
My knees are pulled up
arms crossed around them
I can't cover my ears
with my hands
I don't move
I stare ahead
I see the toilet seat is up

If I scream
the children will hear
If I scream I won't stop
If you were a better wife
I wouldn't have to do this
he says, and then
Do you agree with me?
Do you? I nod
Say it. I say it
If I was a better wife
you wouldn't have to
do this to me.

Do you want a towel?
I don't —
the breeze through
the open window has
dried me off
Yes, I whisper
He wets the towel
in the shower
twists the corner
flicks my left breast with it
just above my heart
Drops the towel
Pick up the towel
he says, and walks away
You are nothing.

THE BROOM

In your absence, I must sweep the leaves —
laburnum leaves, dead on the porch.

Sweep them all
                down the sunlit stairs.

I know this,
but can't decide which broom to buy.

At the hardware store, Old Frank
stacks rat poison
                next to the finch-feeders,
alongside the squirrel-baffles.

You'll want all three, he proffers dryly,
his tongue scraping birdseed husks
                from gaps between his teeth.

And a broom, I tell him, *nothing flimsy,*
not a one-time broom.

In the garden aisle,
by eight tall rakes
        & sacks of organic mulch

hang seven brooms,
                upright or angled —

I cannot decide which broom to buy.

At home, I unwrap the baffle, the feeder,
the poison, attach baffle to feeder
to a hook
              and hang them
              on a tree.

Wedged between
              the slats of the stairs
lies a stray pellet of poison.

I sit on the porch, waiting, naked —
save for a wide-brimmed hat
to shade   the evening sun.

I listen for your footfall,
      hear only the wind —

          how it troubles
the unswept leaves.

SOMEDAY I'LL LOVE CLARE CHU

after Ocean Vuong, Someday I'll Love Ocean Vuong

Clare, don't be afraid.
A box of chocolates is only
a box of chocolates.
Clare, you can eat them all yourself
if you want,
or offer one or two to your friends —
or not.
You do not have to count them.
There is no fair share here.

If you want to wear a scarlet corset,
trimmed with black lace.
If you want to stand and admire your reflection,
go buy a full-length mirror
with a dark wood frame —
position it across from your bed.
Outside strip naked under the desert moon
and step into the corset.
Step through the French doors
into your bedroom.
And look at yourself for a very long time.

Clare, buy flowers every Saturday
at the market
for yourself.
When the florist says, *you always choose
the most beautiful flowers,
you must really love the person
you buy them for,*
just smile and say,
*I do.
Yes, I do.*

ACKNOWLEDGMENTS

My children — India, Naomi and Axel — have, simultaneously, given me space and stood at my side since the beginning. They have helped in numerous ways, large and small, and often without realizing they are doing so. I couldn't ask for more.

I continue to be inspired by the paintings and calligraphic works of The Master of the Water, Pine and Stone Retreat, whose mentorship in all areas of my life has been a treasured gift to me over the many years of our always-evolving and close friendship.

I would like to thank Henry G. Stanton for his unwavering faith in me, his flexibility and his patience, as my poems found their home in this book.

I would like to thank Tony Barnstone and Cecilia Woloch for taking time out of their busy schedules to read my manuscript and agree to write blurbs for this book.

Above all others, I am deeply grateful to my close friend and fellow poet, Chris (C. W. Emerson), who has shown me how to lift poetry from the mundane world, and who continues to challenge my work with a grace and kindness rarely found today. His intuitive ability to critique my poems, while remaining empathetic, has given me the freedom to express myself in a profound way that I didn't understand was possible, and for that I thank him beyond measure.

NOTES

The Phrase **"A LIFETIME, KNEELING"** is adapted from a line in Forugh Farroukhzad's poem *"Wind-Up Doll"* (translated by Sholeh Wolpe).

The phrase **"THE END OF THE ROAD, SO FAR AHEAD"** is adapted from a line in Ocean Vuong's poem *"Someday I'll Love Ocean Vuong"*.

FIRST LINES   Foot notes:
1.   Daphne du Maurier. *Last night I dreamt I went to Manderley again*
2.   Sylvia Plath. *I shut my eyes and all the world drops dead*

3.   Emily Dickinson. *Death is a Dialogue between the Spirit and the Dust*
4.   Patti Smith. *I can not walk*
5.   Leonard Cohen. *Give me back my broken night*

THE CLOUDS SEND DOWN RAIN was written for The Master of the Water, Pine and Stone Retreat.

Some phrases in **THE FALCON MUMMY** are taken from lines in Pablo Neruda's poem *"One Hundred Love Sonnets: XVII"* (translated by Mark Eisner).

SNOWBOUND IN JERUSALEM was written for Joseph Baruch Silver.

Clare Chu was raised in Malta and England, and has adopted Palm Springs, CA. as her home. She is an art curator, dealer, lecturer and writer who has authored and published numerous books and academic articles on Asian art. Her poetry is featured in a continuing collaboration with Hong Kong-based calligraphic and landscape painter, The Master of the Water, Pine and Stone Retreat, in which poet and artist challenge and expand traditional media boundaries. Clare is presently working on a collaborative manuscript with the poet, C. W. Emerson.